THE ULTIMATE GUIDE

TO

THE METAPHYSICS OF GOD

FOR

AQA A LEVEL PHILOSOPHY

PAPER TWO

2019 EDITION

PHILOSOPHY ULTIMATE GUIDES SERIES

COPYRIGHT NOTICE

First Kindle Edition 2019
First Paperback Edition 2020
© 2020 Tristan Elby
All rights reserved.

This textbook is the original work of the author.

No part of this publication may be reproduced, distributed, or transmitted in any form or by any means, including photocopying, recording, or other electronic or mechanical methods, without the prior written permission of the author, except in the case of brief quotations embedded in critical reviews and certain other noncommercial uses permitted by copyright law.

PREFACE

This book will seem a little odd compared to other textbooks. You will not find any 'thought points' in boxes in this book. There are no biographies of philosophers, no 'amusing' anecdotes about Aquinas or Kant, and no tiresome 'extension' questions. You will be relieved to know that this is the wordiest section of the entire book - and you'll lose nothing at all if you skip it!

As a teacher of A Level Philosophy, I always wanted to have a textbook that would have all of the details needed for a high-level answer, with no distractions. This is my first attempt at writing such a thing. The basic idea of the 'Ultimate Guide' (T.M.) is that it's as detailed and accurate as a full textbook should be, but as short and to the point as a revision guide. Therefore, you should hopefully find it useful throughout the year in class and for essay-writing, as well as during revision time.

This book isn't a 'teach yourself' book; it assumes you have access to a class and a teacher where you'll have the verbal discussions that lead to understanding the basic thrust of an argument.

My idea is that if you have an essay due the next day, or if you're revising for a test or exam, you don't need a long explanation of each argument. You've already gone through the explanations and analysis in class, and hopefully that's equipped you with a broad, general, understanding of each argument or idea. What you probably need the most at that point is a series of bullet points that allow you to memorise the key details to hit in your essay, and to present these key details in a logical order.

I hope I've achieved that goal. If you have any improvements to suggest, or you'd like to send any comments or questions, I'd love to hear from you. You can email me at:

tristan.elby@cantab.net

In time, I'll write a separate book for each of the other three topics on the AQA syllabus. Metaphysics of Mind is the next on my list. If you're taking exams in May 2021, I wish you the absolute best of luck and I hope this book helps you in some way with studying and revision.

Tristan Elby
June 2020

Contents

1. **THE CONCEPT AND NATURE OF "GOD"** 6
   - 1.1 GOD AS OMNISCIENT, OMNIPOTENT, AND SUPREMELY GOOD 7
   - 1.2 GOD AS ETERNAL AND GOD AS EVERLASTING 8
     - 1.2.1 TIMELESS (ETERNAL) 8
     - 1.2.2 WITHIN TIME (EVERLASTING) 9
   - 1.3 ARGUMENTS FOR THE INCOHERENCE OF THE CONCEPT OF GOD 10
     - 1.3.1 THE PARADOX OF THE STONE 10
     - 1.3.2 THE EUTHYPHRO DILEMMA 12
     - 1.3.3 OMNISCIENCE AND FREE WILL 14
2. **ARGUMENTS RELATING TO THE EXISTENCE OF GOD** 16
   - 2.1 THE ONTOLOGICAL ARGUMENT 17
     - 2.1.1 ST ANSELM'S ONTOLOGICAL ARGUMENT 17
     - 2.1.2 DESCARTES' ONTOLOGICAL ARGUMENT 20
     - 2.1.3 NORMAL MALCOLM'S ONTOLOGICAL ARGUMENT 22
     - 2.1.4 HUME'S OBJECTIONS TO THE ONTOLOGICAL ARGUMENT 24
     - 2.1.5 KANT'S OBJECTION TO THE ONTOLOGICAL ARGUMENT 26
   - 2.2 THE TELEOLOGICAL ARGUMENT 27
     - 2.2.1 THE DESIGN ARGUMENT FROM ANALOGY 27
     - 2.2.2 WILLIAM PALEY'S DESIGN ARGUMENT 30
     - 2.2.3 RICHARD SWINBURNE'S DESIGN ARGUMENT 32
     - 2.2.4 OTHER OBJECTIONS TO THE DESIGN ARGUMENT 34
   - 2.3 THE COSMOLOGICAL ARGUMENT 35
     - 2.3.1 THE KALĀM COSMOLOGICAL ARGUMENT 35
     - 2.3.2 AQUINAS' COSMOLOGICAL ARGUMENT 38
     - 2.3.3 DESCARTES' COSMOLOGICAL ARGUMENT 40
     - 2.3.4 LEIBNIZ' COSMOLOGICAL ARGUMENT 41
     - 2.3.5 CRITICISMS OF THE COSMOLOGICAL ARGUMENT 42
   - 2.4 THE PROBLEM OF EVIL 44
     - 2.4.1 THE NATURE OF EVIL 44
     - 2.4.2 THE LOGICAL AND EVIDENTIAL PROBLEMS OF EVIL 44
     - 2.4.3 THE FREE WILL DEFENCE (ALVIN PLANTINGA) 46
     - 2.4.4 THE SOUL-MAKING THEODICY (JOHN HICK) 49

3. RELIGIOUS LANGUAGE 52
3.1 COGNITIVISM VS NON-COGNITIVISM IN RELIGIOUS LANGUAGE 53
3.2.1 VERIFICATIONISM 54
3.2.2 ESCHATOLOGICAL VERIFICATION 57
3.3 THE UNIVERSITY DEBATE 60
3.3.1 FLEW: FALSIFICATION AND THE GARDENER 60
3.3.2 MITCHELL: THE PARTISAN AND THE STRANGER 62
3.3.3 HARE: BLIKS AND THE LUNATIC 64
4. NOTES AND REFERENCES 66

1. THE CONCEPT AND NATURE OF "GOD"

1.1 GOD AS OMNISCIENT, OMNIPOTENT, AND SUPREMELY GOOD

General note: An attribute is a quality or characteristic of something. Our concept of God comes from God's attributes.

Why the attributes of God are important

The three 'omni' attributes are what makes up the "God of Classical Theism". This term means the god that Christians traditionally worship.

If Philosophy demonstrates that God doesn't have all of these attributes, then He is not the God of Classical Theism, and in that case, He either doesn't exist or is not the God that Christians worship.

Therefore, a genuine problem with any attribute basically disproves the existence of the Christian god.

The attributes – Basic definitions

Omniscient: God is all-knowing. He knows everything that can possibly be known. God's knowledge is complete and perfect.

Omnipotent: God is all-powerful. He has unlimited power and can bring about anything he chooses.

Supremely good (omnibenevolent): God is all-loving. He is supremely good because He has perfect good will to all of His creation.

(See 1.3 for the problems with these attributes.)

1.2 GOD AS ETERNAL AND GOD AS EVERLASTING

General note: The God of Classical Theism definitely didn't begin to exist and will never cease to exist. The following are essentially two different ways of explaining how this could work.

1.2.1 TIMELESS (ETERNAL)

Basic definition of God as Timeless: God is atemporal. This means that God does not exist in time at all. God is outside time. God has no beginning or end because these concepts only apply to things that are in time.

Strength: Seeing God as eternal makes it much easier to see God as immutable, since change is only possible in time. It also makes it much easier to explain how God could know the future without the future being pre-determined.

Problems with this definition and potential replies

Problem: If God is outside time, God could not possibly act in time. All action happens at a particular time, and God is not part of time at all. Therefore, God cannot respond to prayers and could not possibly have incarnated as Jesus two thousand years ago.
Therefore, this definition could not be of the Christian God of Classical Theism.

Reply: God's actions are not in time, but the effects of those actions are. Hence, God acts atemporally, but the effects occur in time without God becoming temporal.

Further problem: The incarnation means that God, an atemporal being, became human at a single point in history. God could not do this and still be an eternal being, as God would then be existing in time as the Son, Jesus.

Reply: Jesus the Son, as the second person of the Trinity, could not become temporal at a certain point. But he could eternally have two natures, one divine and one human. At some points the human nature of Jesus becomes temporally actual without God becoming temporal.

1.2.2 WITHIN TIME (EVERLASTING)

Basic definition of God as Everlasting: God exists within time. God has no beginning or end because God has existed for all of time so far and will exist forever into the future.

Strength: Seeing God as everlasting is more consistent with Biblical evidence. In the Psalms God is described as 'everlasting', and in other parts of The Old Testament God is described as becoming angry. On a common sense reading this would imply God is in time.

Problems with this definition and potential replies

Problem: An everlasting being in time would not be a perfect being because it would exist only in the present, which is fleeting. The past does not exist any longer and the future does not exist yet.

To be a perfect being, God must exist in the fullest sense possible. God would be greater if God possessed all the moments of His life at once, as He would if He were eternal.

Reply: It is impossible and incoherent for a being to exist other than in the present. God cannot be expected to exist in a way that does not make sense.

Problem from Aquinas: Time is a succession of changes. If a being were completely immutable, it would have no changes so it wouldn't be in time.

Therefore: God is either not immutable or he is not everlasting. God as a perfect being must be immutable so He cannot be everlasting and in time.

1.3 ARGUMENTS FOR THE INCOHERENCE OF THE CONCEPT OF GOD

General Note

Incoherence is a logical term. It means than a claim does not make sense, perhaps because it contains two ideas that conflict with each other.

Each of the three bullet points in the syllabus is a different way of showing that the concept of God does not make sense.

1.3.1 THE PARADOX OF THE STONE

If God is all powerful, he ought to be able to do anything. If he couldn't, he wouldn't be all-powerful because there would be something he didn't have the power to do.

If there were a stone that God couldn't lift, He wouldn't be all-powerful.

If there were an object that God couldn't create, He wouldn't be all-powerful.

If God is able to create any object, He ought to be able to create a stone that He couldn't lift.

If God could do this, then there would be something He couldn't lift, which would mean He would not be omnipotent.

If God couldn't do this, then there would be something He couldn't create, which would mean He wouldn't be omnipotent.

Either God can create such a stone or He can't. There is no middle option. Either way He is not omnipotent.

Therefore: An Omnipotent God does not exist.

Reply to the paradox

God can only do the logically possible. He cannot create a square circle or anything else that doesn't make sense.

Since God is all-powerful, the concept of a stone too heavy for Him as an all-powerful being to lift does not make sense.

Therefore: God cannot be expected to create something that doesn't even make sense as a concept. To expect Him to be able to create such a stone is no more logical than expecting Him to be able to create a square circle.

1.3.2 THE EUTHYPHRO DILEMMA

A dilemma is a question with only two possible answers. Socrates poses the Euthyphro dilemma in a dialogue written by Plato. It only has two possible answers, and each answer is difficult to accept if you believe in the God of Classical Theism.

The Dilemma: Does God command us to behave ethically because behaving ethically is good regardless of God, or is it good to behave ethically just because God has commanded it?

First Possible Answer: Behaving ethically is good regardless of what God commands. This means that what is good is independent of God.

This possible answer is a problem for God's omnipotence. It implies that God can't control what is good and bad. Good and bad are an independent part of reality.

Therefore: If this is the case, God is not all-powerful, because there is a part of reality He can't control. So omnipotence is not true.

Second Possible Answer: Behaving ethically is good just because God commands us to behave this way. This implies that whatever God commands is good, and the good is arbitrary – whatever God wants it to be.

If the good is whatever God wants it to be, then it adds nothing to the concept of God to say that he is supremely good. He is just whatever He is. So omnibenevolence does not make sense.

If what is good is arbitrary (based on God's whim), then it could change tomorrow. God cannot justly punish or reward us.

Therefore: On this possible answer, God's supreme goodness is trivial, and there can be no just punishments or rewards for our actions. Neither is acceptable for normal Christian beliefs.

Alston's reply to the Euthyphro Dilemma: Accept that God is the source of goodness

Explaining goodness will always involve a point where no further explanation is looked for. There must be a stopping point.

It is no more arbitrary to say that God is the source of goodness than to say that an independent Realm of Forms is, as Plato does. In both cases explanation stops right there.

Therefore: There is nothing wrong with the second possible answer above. It just is the case that God is necessarily good, and He is the supreme standard of goodness.

It is not unjust for God to reward or punish us accordingly, or, at least, it is no more unjust than if He punished us because of a God-independent standard of goodness.

1.3.3 OMNISCIENCE AND FREE WILL

The Problem

If God knows everything, then he knows all facts about the past, present, and future.

Knowledge is justified, true, belief. If someone knows something (as opposed to just believes it) then it is true.

If God knows the future, the future must already be true.

If the future is already true, then we don't have a choice about our actions because what we are going to do is already determined.

If we don't have a choice about our actions we do not have free will.

Therefore: Either we don't have free will (and thus we can't be justly punished or rewarded for our actions), or God is not omniscient (because he doesn't know the future).

Neither possibility is acceptable for normal Christian beliefs.

Reply - God knows the future atemporally

If God is eternal, He does not know the future before it happens. He knows the past, present, and future simultaneously, from outside time.

This means that the future is not true before it happens – it's only known to God from outside time.

Therefore: We still have free will because what we will do in the future is not yet true within time, so determinism is not true.

Note: See the God as Eternal section at 1.2 for problems with this reply.

2. ARGUMENTS RELATING TO THE EXISTENCE OF GOD

2.1 THE ONTOLOGICAL ARGUMENT

2.1.1 ST ANSELM'S ONTOLOGICAL ARGUMENT

Basic features

Deductive: Anselm proves God's existence via reasoning that, if valid and based on sound premises, leads to a certain conclusion. If you accept his premises and logic, you must accept his conclusion.

A priori: Anselm's argument is based only on logic and the meanings of words. It does not involve observations of the universe.

Reductio ad absurdum: Anselm's argument works by proving that it is absurd to deny the existence of God. It proves God's existence in reverse – not by giving reasons to believe in God, but by showing that it doesn't make sense to deny God's existence.

Basic argument (sometimes called his first argument, found in Proslogion II)

God is a being than which nothing greater can be conceived. This is the definition of the word 'God'.

Even people who don't believe in God (such as the 'fool' mentioned in the Bible) accept this definition.

God exists in the understanding, even in the understanding of someone who denies that He exists. The fool accepts that God exists in the fool's understanding.

God is a being a greater than which nothing can be conceived, so He can't just exist in the understanding, because then a greater being could be conceived: one that exists in reality too.

Thus, it is absurd and logically contradictory to accept that God is a being a greater than which cannot be conceived, but to deny that He exists in reality.

Therefore: Since God does exist in the understanding, God must certainly exist in reality as well as in the understanding.

Anselm's development of his argument (sometimes called his second argument, found in Proslogion III)

It is possible to conceive a being which cannot even be conceived not to exist.

Such a being would be greater than a being that can be conceived not to exist.

Hence, a being that is a greater than which cannot be conceived, must be a being that cannot be conceived not to exist.

Anything else that exists other than this being can be conceived not to exist.

Therefore: God exists necessarily (e.g., He must exist and cannot be conceived not to exist), and He is unique in existing in this way among everything else that exists.

Gaunilo's "Perfect Island" objection

Imagine a mythical island said to be the best possible island, with all possible riches and abundance.

Such an island is easily understandable as a concept, so it exists in the understanding.

By the same logic as Anselm uses, it can be proven to exist: the best possible island would be one that existed in reality as well as the understanding, or else it wouldn't be the best possible island, and we have already accepted that the best possible island exists in the understanding.

It is obvious that the best possible island cannot be proved to exist in this way; a perfect anything could thus be proved to exist, no matter how nonsensical.

The fact that Anselm's reasoning leads to a ridiculous conclusion shows that the reasoning is faulty. This demonstrates that you cannot prove the existence of God in this way.

(Note: Gaunilo agrees with Anselm that God exists, and couldn't possibly not exist. He just argues that Anselm's method of proving it doesn't work.)

Anselm's response to Gaunilo

Anselm demonstrates in Proslogion III that God is a necessary being.

In the *Responsio*, Anselm argues that he is not presenting an argument that could possibly apply to contingent thing like an island.

Therefore: The ontological argument can only apply to a single, unique, being, a greater than which cannot be conceived, so it cannot be reduced to absurdity in the way that Gaunilo tries to do.

Note: Anselm directly responded to Gaunilo's criticism in his *Responsio*.

2.1.2 DESCARTES' ONTOLOGICAL ARGUMENT

Important definition

Clear and distinct ideas: Ideas that we can be certain about just by examining them in our minds. We do not need any empirical experience to be certain about these ideas. Examples are "I exist", the concept of what God is, and basic truths of mathematics and logic.

When we meditate on these ideas, they are self-evident and we understand they are certainly true (according to Descartes).

Basic Argument

In my thoughts I have various ideas of things which I perceive clearly and distinctly. This includes geometric shapes such as triangles.

The properties that I perceive these things to have are certain. It is certain that the angles of a triangle add up to 180 degrees, even though it is possible that no triangles actually exist.

I have an idea of God, a supremely perfect being. This idea I perceive as clearly and distinctly as I do a triangle. I cannot imagine that God is anything other than a supremely perfect being, just as I cannot imagine a triangle to not have three sides.

Existence is a perfection. Because it is a perfection, it is inherent to the idea of God, a supremely perfect being.

It is impossible to conceive of God without existence, just as it is impossible to conceive of a mountain without a valley, or a triangle whose angles don't add up to 180 degrees.

Therefore: God must really exist; it is impossible to imagine Him not existing.

Criticisms of Descartes' argument

(a) Our idea of God is not a clear and distinct perception

Descartes' argument relies on his theory of clear and distinct perceptions to support the idea that existence is inseparable from the concept of God, and that God is unique in this. However, it is unclear whether we really do have such a clear and distinct perception.

Our concept of God is much more likely to come from our cultural background, and we have no reason to trust that this concept must be the way it is, or that it's true.

If the concept of God is not a clear and distinct perception, then anything, such as a perfect island, could be arbitrarily said to have existence as part of its essence, making Descartes vulnerable to objections like Gaunilo's.

(b) There is still no reason to believe that God really does exist outside our thoughts

A philosopher called Caterus argued that, even if Descartes is right that existence is inseparable from the concept of God, this is still just a fact about our mental life, not the real world.

It's still possible there is no God, even though, if there were a God, His existence would be part of his essence. Descartes still cannot bridge the gap between our thoughts and reality.

2.1.3 NORMAL MALCOLM'S ONTOLOGICAL ARGUMENT

Important definition

Necessary: Something that must be the case and cannot be imagined not to be the case. It is necessarily true that triangles have three corners.

Basic Argument

God is a being a greater than which cannot be conceived. He is unlimited, both in terms of what He can do, and in terms of His existence.

If God does not exist than he cannot come into existence. If God came into existence, either by accident or because He had a cause, He would be limited and dependent. This would go against His definition as an unlimited being.

If God cannot come into existence, then if He doesn't exist His existence is impossible.

If God does exist, He cannot stop existing and cannot have come into existence at some point, again because this would make Him limited and dependent.

If God exists, His existence is therefore necessary.

Hence, God's existence is either logically impossible or logically necessary.

The concept of God is not self-contradictory or logically absurd, so His existence can't be impossible.

Therefore: God necessarily exists.

Key strength of Malcolm's argument

Malcolm does not rely on claiming that it is somehow greater to exist than to not exist, so he avoids objections such as Kant's that show that existence does not add anything to a concept.

Additionally, he relies on a simple, plausible, conception of God as a being unlimited with regard to His existence.

Criticism of Malcolm's argument

Davies argues that Malcolm confuses two types of impossibility. It is true that if God does not exist in our world, He could not come into existence because then He would be limited. But that wouldn't make His existence logically impossible. It would just make His existence impossible as a contingent matter of fact.

To make his argument work, Malcolm needs it to be the case that God's existence could only be either logically impossible or logically necessary. Therefore, Davies' criticism undermines a key premise of Malcom's argument.

2.1.4 HUME'S OBJECTIONS TO THE ONTOLOGICAL ARGUMENT

David Hume - Important background

Hume objects to a priori arguments in general, including the cosmological and ontological arguments.

This is based on his empiricist belief that a priori reasoning can only establish truths about logic or maths (he calls this 'relations of ideas', modern philosophers call this 'analytic' truth).

For Hume, knowledge about the real world (he calls this 'matters of fact', modern philosophers call this 'synthetic' truth) must come from empirical evidence.

In a nutshell, without empirical evidence, all you have is geometry, maths, logic, and word definitions. You'll never prove what actually exists.

Hume Objection 1: It is impossible to prove that anything exists a priori

Nothing is true a priori (Hume calls this 'demonstrable'), unless the contrary implies a contradiction. E.g., it is true a priori (or 'demonstrable') that a triangle has three sides, because it would be logically contradictory to say 'A triangle has two sides.'

Anything we can clearly conceive to exist can be clearly conceived not to exist.

If we can clearly conceive the non-existence of something, it can't be logically contradictory.

Therefore: There is no being whose non-existence would be logically contradictory, so there is no being that can be proved to exist by an a priori argument, like the ontological argument.

Hume Objection 2: The concept of necessary existence is meaningless
If a being were necessarily existent, we would find it impossible to imagine it not existing, just as it is impossible to imagine 2 + 2 not being 4.

In the case of 2 + 2 = 4 our minds necessarily have to conceive this to be true. It is impossible for our minds to be under such a necessity for objects or beings in the real world, because we can always imagine their non-existence.

Whatever qualities that would supposedly make God necessarily existent if we understood His nature perfectly, are therefore completely unknown and unimaginable, and in any case, could equally apply to the universe itself, since they are unknown and unimaginable.

Therefore: It is meaningless to refer to any being as necessarily existent - the idea does not make sense.

2.1.5 KANT'S OBJECTION TO THE ONTOLOGICAL ARGUMENT

Kant's argument

A predicate is the part of a sentence that describes the subject.

Saying "God is omnipotent" attributes the predicate of omnipotence to the subject, God.

Saying "There is a God" doesn't attribute any predicate to God. It merely says that the concept of God with all its predicates really exists as an object.

The concept of 100 Thalers (Prussian currency) is not made greater or increased by their really existing as an object. 100 Thalers is 100 Thalers whether it exists in reality or not.

Existence does not add anything to the concept of something. Therefore, existence is not a predicate.

Because existence is not a predicate, the concept of God is not greater for existing in reality.

Therefore: This undermines a key premise of Anselm's argument. For Anselm's argument to work, it must be greater to exist in reality than the understanding.

2.2 THE TELEOLOGICAL ARGUMENT

General features of teleological / design arguments

They present an *a posteriori* argument for God's existence. This means they rely upon empirical observations to support their conclusion.

Even if they are successful arguments, they demonstrate that God's existence is probable, but not certain. It is the best explanation for our observations, but even the people making the arguments accept that the conclusion could be false, even if it's unlikely.

Therefore, unlike the ontological argument, they do not establish that God exists necessarily. If He exists, it is just a contingent fact about our particular universe.

2.2.1 THE DESIGN ARGUMENT FROM ANALOGY

Basic features

Hume presents this argument thoroughly in order to refute it. It is presented as a dialogue between a sceptical character who represents Hume and two religious characters who present arguments for God's existence.

It is an argument from analogy because it is based on two different things resembling each other. This resemblance is used to draw an analogy between them to support the idea that the cause of one must be the same as the cause of the other.

Argument

The natural world displays great complexity; it resembles a machine subdivided into many smaller machines. Such machines appear to be adjusted to work together with each other with great accuracy.

The way that things in the natural world are adapted to serve a variety of purposes resembles the what is produced by human design and intelligence. In fact, it appears to far exceed human capabilities.

If the effects in one case resemble the effects in another case, we should infer that the causes in both cases resemble each other.

Because of its resemblance to things designed by human intelligence, the cause of the natural world must also be an intelligent being, possessing much greater intelligence and capabilities than Humanity.

This being is God, who is the intelligent creator of the world.

Hume's objections to the design argument from analogy

Objection 1

The cause we infer must be proportional to the effect: If we find that one side of a scale is raised and holds a weight of 10 ounces, we can infer that there must be more than 10 ounces on the other side, but can't infer there must be 100 ounces.

With the universe, we can infer that it was created by something capable of producing order, but we can't infer that it's God, especially not an omnipotent, omniscient, omnibenevolent God.

Objection 2

If one type of object has always been observed to occur with another type of object, we can infer the existence of one from the existence of the other.

In the teleological argument, we have never observed a god, so we can't leap from the existence of order to the existence of a god.

You have to have observed both types of objects before in order to infer one from the other.

Objection 3

If a mind created the universe, that mind itself would need explaining just as much as our universe needs explaining. It is not satisfactory to explain one mystery with another mystery.

Therefore, the teleological argument does not provide a satisfactory explanation for the origin of the universe.

Objection 4 (The epicurean hypothesis)

The matter in the universe is continually rearranging itself. Over a vast amount of time it is bound to eventually arrange itself in an ordered manner for a temporary period.

The simplest explanation of our experience of order is that we live in one of the brief ordered periods of the matter in the universe.

Objection 5
If we are drawing an analogy with human creations, it would be logical to assume that the deity has a body, face, and other human characteristics.

This is self-evidently ridiculous, and shows that the teleological argument fails to argue from a good analogy.

2.2.2 WILLIAM PALEY'S DESIGN ARGUMENT

Basic features

Spatial order: Things being ordered in terms of their arrangement – like parts arranged to serve a purpose. This is spatial because the order comes from how the parts are placed.

Argument

If we found a stone on a heath we would not seek to explain its existence in terms of a maker; it could have just been there forever. Conversely, if we came upon a watch, we would infer that it had a maker who designed it.

We would think this about the watch and not the stone because the watch has properties displaying order and purpose:
  - it has complex parts carefully arranged together for a purpose
  - its parts could not be re-arranged or altered in shape and size without removing the watch's ability to serve that purpose
  - its parts are made of specific materials necessary to serve its purpose

Elements of the natural world have all the properties displaying order and purpose that a watch would display. For example, human eyes have precisely arranged lenses and membranes designed to focus light in a way that enables humans to see at both short and long distances.

The very close resemblance between natural objects such as eyes and human artefacts such as telescopes or watches means that we should conclude that natural objects are designed - they display evidence of order and purpose even more than human artefacts do.

There cannot be design without a designer.

Therefore: We can conclude that a designer exists, and this designer is God.

Hume on the Problem of Spatial Disorder

The world and the universe contain many examples of disorder and entropy. These persist for long stretches of time. Matter is often corrupt and the universe can contain irregular motion for long periods.

In our minds, disorder is often present in the form of madness.

Therefore: There is no reason to think that the universe as a whole contains enough order to require a divine creator as an explanation.

Paley's response to the Problem of Spatial Disorder

The fact that a watch went wrong sometimes, or even that it was a bit inaccurate most of the time, wouldn't change the fact that it had clear evidence of purpose and design.

Even if a watch we found had superfluous parts which we were certain didn't contribute to any purpose, we would still be reasonable to conclude that, overall, it had a design.

Therefore: In the same way, the fact that there is disorder in the universe and parts of it don't have any clear purpose doesn't change the fact that there is clear evidence of design for parts of it, and this still implies a designer.

2.2.3 RICHARD SWINBURNE'S DESIGN ARGUMENT

Basic features

Temporal order: Things being ordered because they display patterns of the same behaviour over time.

For example, Newton's Law of Gravity describes the way that bodies in space always attract each other with a force proportional to their masses.

This is temporal order because this order is observed repeatedly over time, rather than an arrangement at one time in space.

Argument

We observe regularities of succession everywhere in the world - almost everything obeys simple natural laws, and almost everything appears to behave in a regular way. This is temporal order.

The most fundamental regularities can't be explained by natural laws. We can't explain why the universe obeys the most fundamental natural laws, other than to say it is a brute fact, which is not an explanation.

The free choice of rational agents is the only way to explain natural phenomena other than through normal scientific explanations. It is accepted that we should resort to explanation in terms of the rational choice of free agents when explaining human choices; we don't explain them in terms of natural laws.

Some regularities of succession can be explained as a result of the free choice of rational agents. For example, the notes of a song sung by a singer display temporal order and are the result of the free choice of the singer.

There is some similarity between regularities of succession produced by humans such as songs, and the regularities of succession not produced by humans such as the action of fundamental natural laws - both show temporal order.

Since we cannot explain fundamental non-human-produced regularities of succession by natural laws, the only other option is to explain them in terms of the rational choice of a free agent.

Such an agent must be of immense power and intelligence, and must act directly on the whole universe at once. Therefore, such an agent could not have a body.

Explaining temporal order by appeal to such an agent is a simple, coherent, explanation for temporal order and is thus consistent with science.

Therefore: The best explanation for the temporal order in the universe is that a very powerful, free, non-embodied, rational agent exists and is responsible for it.

2.2.4 OTHER OBJECTIONS TO THE DESIGN ARGUMENT

The design argument fails as it is an argument from a unique case (Hume)

The universe is a unique object. We have observed many ships and cities being built, and thus we can infer that it came from a designer or designers if we find a ship or city.

But we have no experience of the origin of universes, so we have no basis for inferring anything about where the universe came from.

Whether God is the best or only explanation

Multiple or senile gods

Even if the teleological argument makes it likely that the world was designed, it is still too uncertain what the designer is like to be a good argument for the existence of God.

There could be multiple designers, for example. We have no other universes for comparison, so it is just as likely that this universe is the product of a young and incompetent designer, or an old and senile one.

This would not be the God of Classical Theism.

No God at all, just organic

Trees are able to bestow order on the trees that spring from their seeds. This is an example of order being created without a designing mind.

The teleological argument argues by analogy from the world, so if the cause of order in the world is often vegetable or animal generation, then it would be reasonable to assume that the universe as a whole came into being by the same sort of process, not the effort of a rational creator.

Therefore: The teleological argument cannot show there is a need to conclude that there is a God, since there could be multiple creators not worthy of worship, or no creator at all.

2.3 THE COSMOLOGICAL ARGUMENT

General features of cosmological arguments

Unlike teleological arguments, cosmological arguments are normally deductive. They present an argument that, if successful, establishes that God certainly exists.

Cosmological arguments are *a posteriori*. They depend on the fact that something exists (an *a posteriori* truth) to infer that there must be a cause of what exists.

Like teleological arguments, cosmological arguments establish God's existence as the creator of the universe, but do not prove that He is perfect or has the qualities of the God of Classical Theism.

2.3.1 THE KALĀM COSMOLOGICAL ARGUMENT

General note
It is an argument from temporal (relating to time) causation because it argues that there must be a point in time that the universe began, and thus a cause that came before the beginning of the universe.

Basic Argument

Anything that begins to exist must have a cause.

It is impossible for an actual infinite to exist.

If the universe had existed forever, it would be an infinite series of events, which is impossible.

Hence, the universe began to exist.

Since the universe began to exist, the universe must have a cause.

There is no scientific explanation of the cause of the beginning of the universe.

Explanations are either scientific (natural laws), or personal (an agent of some sort making a choice).

Since there is no scientific explanation, the cause must be a personal agent.

Therefore: A personal God exists and is the cause of the universe.

Whether an infinite series is possible

Definition: A paradox is a problem that has no solution. It is a contradiction. If a concept (like an infinite series) leads to a paradox, the concept does not make sense and thus cannot be possible.

Basic argument

Craig argues that the universe must have begun at some point in time, because otherwise it would stretch back infinitely in time, and this is impossible.

It is impossible because an infinite series of anything is impossible, including moments of time. We know that an infinite series is impossible because it leads to absurd paradoxes such as the Hilbert's Hotel situation that Craig explains:

Hilbert's Hotel Paradox

Imagine a hotel with an infinite number of rooms. Suppose that every room was full. It should be impossible to accept a new guest.

However, the owner could just shift every existing guest to a room numbered one higher than before. E.g., the guest in room 1 to room 2, 2 to 3, and so on. Thus, room 1 would be empty, and a new guest could be accommodated in a full hotel without removing any of the existing guests.

It doesn't make sense that a full hotel could accommodate a new guest without removing one of the existing guests. This is a contradiction.

If actually infinite things lead to contradictions, then it is not possible that there could be an actual infinite. We can talk about infinity as an idea, but an infinite number of things couldn't exist in reality.

Therefore: The universe could not have existed for an infinite amount of time in the past.

An objection from other mathematicians

The library and hotel examples are based on a mistake. The mistake is to use mathematical concepts that are appropriate for finite numbers (bigger or smaller than, for example) on infinity. Mathematicians like Cantor have developed ways of thinking about infinite sets of things that are now an established part of mathematics.

Therefore: there is no contradiction or paradox in an actual infinite series, so the universe could be infinitely old, and thus not have a beginning that would require a cause.

Final Note: If the hotel example is difficult to remember, Craig also gives the example of a library with an infinite number of books.

Library Books Paradox

The infinite library contains an infinite number of red books and an infinite number of black books. For every red book the library has a black book.

Since the library has an infinite number of red books, it has the same number of red books as the entire collection of books, both red and black.

This is ridiculous. The red books are a smaller part (a subset) of the whole library. They cannot be the same size as the entire library, and yet they would have to be, since both the library and the red books are infinite.

If the collection of red books is simultaneously the same size as the whole library and smaller than it, this is a contradiction.

The paradox thus shows that an actual infinite is not possible.

2.3.2 AQUINAS' COSMOLOGICAL ARGUMENT

The First Way (Motion)
It is certain that some things in the world are in motion.

Motion is a change from potentiality to actuality. Nothing can be simultaneously in potentiality and actuality, so nothing can change itself from potentiality to actuality.

Hence, nothing can be in motion unless it is set in motion by another mover (something already in actuality).

Without a first mover, there would be no movers at all. Hence, there cannot be an infinite series of movers.

Therefore: There must be a first mover, which was not put in motion by any other. This is God.

The Second Way (Atemporal causation)

Important definition

Efficient cause: The efficient cause of an object is some other object or objects which directly start the movement or change that produces the object.

Argument

There is clearly a sequence of efficient causes in the world.

Nothing can be the efficient cause of itself, otherwise it would precede itself in time, which is impossible.

If there were no first cause in the sequence of efficient causes, there would be no intermediate or ultimate causes.

Hence, there cannot be an infinite series of efficient causes.

Therefore: There must be a first efficient cause, and this is God.

The Third Way (Contingency)
There are contingent things in nature whose non-existence is possible.

If all things were contingent then at some point nothing would have existed.

If nothing existed at some point, then it would have been impossible for anything to begin to exist.

Hence, there must exist something whose existence is necessary.

There cannot be an infinite number of necessary things all causing each other.

Therefore: There must be a being whose necessity comes from itself, which is God.

2.3.3 DESCARTES' COSMOLOGICAL ARGUMENT

General note: Descartes' argument is sometimes called the "Trademark argument". It is a cosmological argument based on causation because it argues from an effect (Descartes existing and having an innate idea of God) to God as the only possible cause of this effect.

Basic Argument

I exist and I clearly conceive an idea of God as an infinite, eternal, perfect, being. This idea is distinct from all other ideas about finite things.

The efficient cause of something must have as much reality as the effect. Otherwise, the effect would not be real.

The idea of God, unlike ideas of people, angels, imaginary creatures, cannot possibly come from my own mind, because I do not have the perfections it contains and I am not infinite.

I cannot have created myself, because I would have given myself all possible knowledge and perfections

There cannot be an infinite regress of causes that led to me, because this would not explain my continuing existence.

My ultimate cause cannot be multiple things, because unity and simplicity is part of the perfection of God, and (as above), the cause must have at least as much reality as the effect.

Therefore: My continued existence as a thinking thing possessing the idea of God can only be explained by the existence of a perfect, necessary, and infinite being which is both the cause and sustainer of my existence.

Final note: *Descartes' argument is not laid out in a clear way in his Meditations. See the notes section for exact references to the AQA Anthology for each premise if you want to read the original.*

2.3.4 LEIBNIZ' COSMOLOGICAL ARGUMENT

Important definition

Contingent: Something that depends on other things for its origins or continued existence. Also something that might not have been the case, or which might not be true in the future.

Basic Argument

For every contingent thing in the world, there is a full explanation (a sufficient reason) for its existence.

To fully explain a contingent thing, you cannot simply trace its contingent causes back to infinity, because then each of those causes would need a full explanation.

The series of causes as a whole, even if it's infinite, needs a full explanation.

Hence, a full explanation for contingent things must come from outside of the sequence of contingent things.

What is outside of the sequence of contingent things would have to be necessary and singular, since it is the full, final, explanation for all particular things.

Therefore: Only one God exists and is a necessary being. God is the sufficient reason for the existence of the universe and everything in it.

Final note: The first premise in the argument is often called the "Principle of Sufficient Reason".

2.3.5 CRITICISMS OF THE COSMOLOGICAL ARGUMENT

Hume's objection to the 'causal principle'

We observe events that consistently happen in the same order and that consistently happen near each other. This is constant conjunction.

From this we infer that one event causes another. This is necessary connection.

The problem is that the necessary connection (a cause and effect relationship) is just an inference. All that we actually observe is constant conjunction.

Hence, it is possible and conceivable that some events don't have a cause.

Therefore: The Cosmological argument is wrong to assume that every event must have a cause.

Russell's criticism using the fallacy of composition

The fallacy of composition is to assume that something must be true about the whole just because it is true of its parts.

Every human has a mother, but this doesn't imply that the human race has a mother.

Just because every thing in the universe has a cause, this doesn't imply that the universe as a whole has a cause.

Therefore: There is no need to conclude that God exists to explain what caused the universe.

Hume and Russell's criticisms of the idea of a necessary being

Hume

"Nothing is demonstrable unless the contrary implies a contradiction." This means that nothing is necessarily true, unless it would be a logical contradiction to deny it.

For example, "A triangle has three sides" is necessarily true, and it is a logical contradiction to say "A triangle has two sides", because the word "triangle" means a shape with three sides.

If we can imagine something, it can't be a logical contradiction (a two sided triangle is impossible to imagine).

Whatever we can imagine to exist, we can imagine not to exist.

Hence, if we can imagine God to exist, we can imagine Him not to exist.

Therefore: If we can imagine God not to exist, He is not a necessary being, because His non-existence does not imply a logical contradiction.

Russell

The word "necessary" can only be applied to analytic propositions like "A triangle has three sides". It cannot be applied to things.

Claiming that a thing or being exists that is necessary does not make sense.

Therefore: The Cosmological Argument is wrong to conclude that a necessary being exists.

2.4 THE PROBLEM OF EVIL

2.4.1 THE NATURE OF EVIL

Moral evil: Evil caused by immoral human choices. Murder, rape, and other crimes, war, and non-criminal but still hurtful acts such as betrayal or viciousness.

Natural evil: Evil caused by events outside of human choice or control. Disease, famine, and disasters such as tsunamis, earthquakes, or hurricanes.

2.4.2 THE LOGICAL AND EVIDENTIAL PROBLEMS OF EVIL

The logical problem of evil

General note: The logical problem of evil is a deductive argument designed to show that if any evil exists at all, the God of Classical Theism cannot exist. Thus, it is based on God's existence being logically incompatible with evil existing.

Argument

It is based on three sentences that can't all be true at the same time, called the Inconsistent Triad:

1. God is omnipotent.
2. God is omnibenevolent.
3. At least some evil exists.

If God were omnipotent and omnibenevolent, he would have the ability and willingness to stop or never allow evil, so 3. would be false.

3. is true (according to those posing the problem) so one or both of 1. or 2. must be false. Either God can't stop evil (not omnipotent) or doesn't want to (not omnibenevolent).

If God lacks just one of omnibenevolence or omnipotence, He is not the God of Classical Theism. Most Christianity is based on belief in the God of Classical Theism, so this is as good as proving that God does not exist.

The evidential problem of evil

General note: The evidential problem of evil is an inductive argument designed to show that it is very unlikely that the God of Classical Theism exists because of the amount or type of evil in the world.

Thus, it shows that God's existence is improbable given the evidence rather than logically incompatible with evil.

Argument

God would prevent any intense suffering He could, as long as He could do so without losing some greater good or allowing some worse evil to happen.

There exists some intense suffering that it is very likely that God could have prevented without losing some greater good or allowing some worse evil to happen.

Therefore: It is very unlikely that God exists, since he has not prevented this intense suffering.

2.4.3 THE FREE WILL DEFENCE (ALVIN PLANTINGA)

General note: Plantinga says that he is only trying to show that there is a logically possible reason why God would permit evil. This is all that is required to disprove the Logical Problem of Evil.

Plantinga's basic argument

God could permit some evil if not permitting it would lead to greater evil or if not permitting it would lose some greater good that outweighs that evil.

The creation of persons with significant free will that voluntarily do good could be such a good that would outweigh the evil caused by the misuse of free will.

Significant free will is where a person can do or refrain from doing things by their own power, without being causally determined. It also requires that they have the ability to do both good and evil actions.

God's omnipotence does not include doing the logically impossible.

It is logically impossible for God to create people with significant free will and simultaneously prevent them from doing evil. Preventing them from doing evil would take away their significant free will.

Hence, it is possible that God cannot prevent evil without losing a greater good.

Therefore: the existence of God is logically compatible with the existence of evil - there are possible reasons why an omnipotent, omniscient, and omnibenevolent God would permit evil.

Problem: Why didn't God create free people who happen to just do good?

If it is logically possible for a free person to freely do nothing but good, it is logically possible for all free beings to freely do nothing but good.

If God is omnipotent, He can create anything logically possible.

Therefore: God cannot be both omnipotent and omnibenevolent because there is a possible world he could have created which is better than the real world.

Plantinga's response - "Transworld depravity"

Important Definition

"Depravity": Wickedness, particularly if it is innate in a person.

Argument

It is logically possible that there could be a free being who commits at least some evil in every possible world. Plantinga calls this "transworld depravity" (being depraved in all possible worlds).

The essence of a person includes the decisions they freely make. Transworld depravity would be part of a person's essence.

God cannot determine the essence of a person (this would be incompatible with free will); He just brings an essence into existence as a real person.

If it is logically possible that one being's essence includes transworld depravity it is logically possible that all beings' essence includes it.

Therefore: It is possible that God couldn't create a world containing free beings without evil, since all free beings would commit at least some evil if their essence included transworld depravity.

Problem: What about natural evil? Natural evil is not the result of the free choices of human beings, so it can't be explained by free will.

Plantinga's responses:

(a) Natural evil leads to moral good

It is possible that some natural evil leads to moral good (e.g., creative responses to evil and hardship, spurring people to greater efforts, etc) in such a way that the universe is in fact better with that evil than without it.

(b) Non-human persons with free will

It is possible that natural evil is due to the free actions of non-human persons.

In the same way as with humans above, it is possible that God could not have created a world with a better balance of good over evil.

The fact that this is possible (even if not likely) means that God's existence is logically compatible with the existence of evil.

Problem: Doesn't the amount of evil make God's existence unlikely?

An omnipotent, omniscient, omnibenevolent God would have created the best of all possible worlds.

The amount of evil makes it very unlikely that this is the best of all possible worlds.

Therefore: it is very unlikely that the God of Classical Theism exists, even if Plantinga has shown it to be logically possible.

Plantinga's responses:

(a) Rejects concept of best of all possible worlds

There is no such thing as a best of all possible worlds. For any imaginable world, more goodness could be added.

Therefore: The criticism doesn't make sense as it is based on there being a best of all possible worlds.

(b) Argument against God's existence being improbable

As in the natural evil response above, all evil is broadly moral evil: it is committed freely by either humans or non-human persons.

It is possible that the actual world contains the best balance of good over evil that is possible for God to create, given transworld depravity.

The amount of evil in the actual world does not make the claim that the actual world contains the best balance of good over evil improbable.

This is because there is no logical connection between any specified amount of evil and it being improbable that God created the world with the best balance of good over evil possible for Him to create.

Therefore: Opponents of the Free Will Defense have not actually provided evidence to make it improbable that God exists.

2.4.4 THE SOUL-MAKING THEODICY (JOHN HICK)

Hick's argument in "Evil and the God of Love":

If a hypnotist implanted suggestions into someone's personality to make them love the hypnotist once they came out of the hypnotic trance, the resulting love would be inauthentic.

It might technically be free because it came from that person's personality and didn't involve external force, but the person would still be basically a puppet and their actions inauthentic.

In the same way, it is not possible that God could make beings who freely respond to Him with love and faith. Such love would be inauthentic and not valuable.

Instead, God would have to create beings with the potential to love him freely. Irenaeus called this being created "in God's image". If such beings achieved this goal, they would have developed into "God's likeness".

The world should be seen as a "vale of soulmaking". This means that it has the right elements for beings to morally and spiritually develop into God's likeness and thus freely love him.

Soulmaking requires a long process of responding freely to "challenges and disciplines". These will inevitably involve pain and suffering. Valuable moral and spiritual character is developed slowly over time.

In a world suitable for soulmaking beings will be at an "epistemic distance" from God. This means that the world is ambiguous so that it is not obvious whether God exists.

If it were obvious that God existed, beings would not freely come to love him or choose to act morally for its own sake. They would feel compelled to do so.

Hence, God has made sure that the world appears to be purely natural, so that if people choose to have faith in him it is a free decision. The distance between humans and God is based on knowledge (e.g., knowledge of whether He exists), so it is an 'epistemic' distance.

Animal suffering contributes to epistemic distance as it appears to be pointless. Hence, it is at least partially justified by the eventual end of the soulmaking process.

The ultimate end of the soulmaking process will be all beings developing, freely, into God's likeness.

Therefore: Evil will ultimately have been vital to creating "infinite good", and God is ultimately justified in permitting it.

Note: *Hick makes this argument over many pages of prose. The above is about as short as I can make it without losing too much detail.*

Problems that Hick responds to

Problem: If God were truly good, He would create a world there were only degrees of pleasure. In this way, we could still use our free will to choose better or worse courses of action, but there would be no pain.

Hick's reply

The scale of pleasure and pain is relative. If God created a world without pain, He would be essentially removing the bottom half (pain) of the scale. In such a world, what is currently the top half (pleasure) of the scale would be the whole of the new scale.

In the new scale, the bottom half of that scale would be called pain, because pain and pleasure are relative.

Therefore: The only way to not have pain would be to have no difference in feeling at all. It is impossible for God to create a world with just degrees of pleasure.

Problem: Even if God couldn't create a soulmaking world without pain, the amount of evil in the world is clearly excessive. God could create a world with enough pain and suffering for soulmaking, but secretly prevent excessive evils, such as the bombing of Hiroshima.

Hick's reply

Evils are only excessive in relation to other evils. If God prevented the nuclear bomb being dropped on Hiroshima, we would see smaller bombings as excessive. If God had secretly prevented the First and Second World Wars, we would see the English and US civil wars as excessive.

Therefore: Unless God eliminated all evils there would always be relatively outstanding evils. Since evil is necessary for soulmaking, God cannot meaningfully change the amount of evil in the world.

Problem: The way that evil is distributed in the world is unjust. Evil appears to be distributed randomly and meaninglessly. People who lead excellent lives often suffer in an undeserved way. If God's intention is soulmaking, evil doesn't actually seem contribute to it.

Hick's reply

Undeserved evil, such as severe natural disasters, provides an opportunity for good such as the development of charity. Without such things, there would be no "uncalculated outpouring" of good in response to disasters.

Also: If the world consistently rewarded good actions and punished bad actions with evil, people would have a self-interested motivation for doing good. Hence, there would be no soulmaking because people would not develop moral characters where they do good for its own sake.

Therefore: The seemingly random or mysterious distribution of evil actually contributes to soulmaking.

3. RELIGIOUS LANGUAGE

General Note

Philosophers seek to explain what religious language means. A successful explanation of what different types of language mean is part of offering a credible overall philosophy.

This a highly 'academic' part of the course because it is more a debate about language than about 'big' questions of whether God exists.

3.1 COGNITIVISM VS NON-COGNITIVISM IN RELIGIOUS LANGUAGE

Cognitivism about religious language

Cognitivists believe that religious language is propositional. This means that it could be factually right or wrong.

Religious language has a truth value. Having a truth value means being true or false.

"God is all-loving." This statement could be potentially proved or disproved, for example by showing that we live in the best of all possible worlds (so it would be true), or by showing that there is too much evil in the world (so it would be false).

Non cognitivism about religious language

Non-cognitivists believe that religious language does not express propositions. It expresses attitudes, intentions, or personal faith.

This means that it has no truth value. It is neither true nor false.

"God is all-loving." This expresses an intention to follow a particular way of life, for example by cultivating an attitude of selfless love. It is a personal intention to live a certain way, so it is neither true nor false.

Final note

Being a non-cognitivist is not the same as being an atheist, and being a cognitivist does not mean being a believer.

Someone posing the logical problem of evil is a cognitivist because they think it's factually meaningful to claim that God exists - they just also think it's false that God exists because of the existence of evil, so they are an atheist as well.

A religious believer could be a non-cognitivist if they think belief is a matter of personal faith rather than something that can be debated using reason.

3.2.1 VERIFICATIONISM

Definition

Logical Positivism: A group of philosophers who believed that all knowledge should be based on publicly verifiable experience together with Mathematics and logical reasoning.

General note

Ayer wanted to limit Philosophy to empirical matters and language by showing that a lot of what philosophers had previously debated was meaningless. He is arguing that the existence or nature of God is not a matter for Philosophy at all.

Ayer is not arguing for atheism or agnosticism. He says that the existence of God is a meaningless concept that Philosophy cannot debate at all. An agnostic would accept that the question is meaningful, even if they don't think it can be answered with our current evidence. Ayer rejects the very question.

Argument

A priori arguments can only have analytic conclusions. If your premises are not based on observation, your conclusion will be a tautology: it will just follow from a definition and will not say anything about the world.

Hence, maths and logic are meaningful, but on their own they cannot tell us anything about the real world. To do this, we need arguments based on synthetic premises.

The verification principle: A sentence is factually meaningful if and only if it expresses a proposition that can be verified empirically.

Sentences about the existence and nature of God are metaphysical. A metaphysical claim cannot be verified empirically.

Hence, religious language is factually meaningless. Sentences about the existence and nature of God are not propositions so they are neither true nor false.

Therefore: All utterances about the existence and nature of God are literally nonsensical, regardless of whether they are asserting or denying the existence of God.

Problem: Some scientific claims cannot be verified empirically but it is ridiculous to say that they are meaningless. For example, many claims about other planets cannot be verified with current technology, but are clearly not meaningless.

Ayer's solution - Distinction between practical verification and verification in principle

A sentence is verifiable in principle, and thus still meaningful, if it is theoretically possible to make observations that would verify it, even if it is not practically possible.

This still excludes religious language because it wouldn't even be theoretically possible to have experience of a non-empirical reality.

Problem: Scientific laws like "A body tends to expand when heated" cannot be fully or conclusively verified because it is always possible that a counterexample will be found in the future. But it would be ridiculous to say that scientific laws are meaningless.

In the same way, sentences about the distant past cannot be fully verified but are clearly not meaningless.

Ayer's solution - Distinction between strong and weak verification

A sentence can be strongly verified if experience can 'conclusively establish' it. It is weakly verifiable if experience could make it probable.

Thus, historical claims are meaningful because experience can make them probable and thus weakly verifiable. The same is true of scientific laws which have been made probable by repeated experience.

Religious language is not meaningful because there are no observations that could even make it probable.

Final criticism of Ayer

Arguments like the design argument may not conclusively establish the existence of God but they are based on observations of the world that are relevant to making His existence probable.

In the same way, detailed observations of religious experiences such as Near Death Experiences (NDEs), Out of Body Experiences (OBEs) and memories of past lives are arguably relevant to the probability of God existing.

Therefore: By allowing weak verification and verification in principle, Ayer has actually allowed sentences about the existence and nature of God to be meaningful.

3.2.2 ESCHATOLOGICAL VERIFICATION

Hick's argument

Claims about existence where it would make no possible difference to our observations whether the claim is true or false are factually meaningless. Hence, Hick accepts verifiability as important.

Religious claims are factual and not just non-cognitive. Hence, they must be verifiable in some way.

It is meaningful if a claim is verifiable but not falsifiable.

The claim that we will have conscious existence after our body dies is verifiable but not falsifiable. If there is no afterlife, there will be no conscious experience at all so the claim will not be falsified. However, li there is an afterlife, the claim will be verified as we will experience it.

Hick uses the "Celestial City" parable: Two men are travelling along a road. One believes that it leads nowhere but it is the only road so he has to travel on it. The other believes that the road leads to a great city called the Celestial city.

They cannot perform any experiment whilst they are on the road to verify or falsify their beliefs, but at the end of the road one of them will be proved right. Hence, they are making factually meaningful claims despite the claims not being verifiable in the present.

Therefore: The religious claim that there is an afterlife is factually meaningful as it is verifiable in principle. At least some religious language is therefore factual and cognitive.

Strength of Hick

Hick's argument is strong because he is defending religious language on Ayer's own terms. He shows that, even if you accept Ayer's Verification Principle, religious language is still verifiable and thus meaningful.

Criticism of Hick

Hick is arguably stretching the meaning of 'verification' too far. In science a claim that can only be verified at death and which can't be reported back to other people is not really verifiable at all.

Therefore: This is a weak response to Ayer that fails to show that religious language is truly verifiable.

3.3 THE UNIVERSITY DEBATE

3.3.1 FLEW: FALSIFICATION AND THE GARDENER

General note: Flew is different to Ayer. For Ayer, no one, believer or atheist, could possibly verify religious language so it is meaningless. For Flew, the way that religious believers refuse to allow their claims to be falsified is what makes them meaningless.

Parable

Two explorers find a clearing in the jungle and disagree about whether there is a gardener maintaining it or not. They stay to find out.

When they don't see a gardener, the believing explorer says he must be invisible. After they patrol with bloodhounds, set up an electric fence and barbed wire, the believing explorer also says that the gardener must not feel electric shocks, not have a scent, not be able to be touched by wire, and make no sound.

The other explorer asks what the difference is between an invisible, intangible, inaudible, gardener and no gardener at all.

The believing explorer's claim about the gardener has become meaningless because he wouldn't allow any evidence to falsify it.

Argument

The parable illustrates how what seems like a reasonable claim can become meaningless and essentially the same as not claiming anything at all. This happens if believers refuse to accept any evidence to falsify their claims.

In religion, Flew argues that a sentence like "God loves us as a father loves his children." is never allowed by believers to be falsified.

Flew gives the example of a child dying of throat cancer. A religious believer would simply qualify their claim by saying God's love is "not like human love" or is an inscrutable (impossible to decipher) sort of love.

Therefore: Religious language suffers a 'death of a thousand qualifications.' So many qualifications are made in response to falsification, that in the end religious claims are not really claiming anything at all.

Criticism of Flew

Flew's argument only works if this is actually how religious believers use language.

In reply, religious believers could argue that the long, 2,000 year old tradition of Theology shows that they take potential falsification much more seriously than that.

Therefore: The explorer's claims about the invisible gardener are an unfair parody of religious language that is not accurate.

3.3.2 MITCHELL: THE PARTISAN AND THE STRANGER

General note: Mitchell is on the side of religious believers. He is arguing in favour of religious language being meaningful in some cases, but he also accepts Flew's point that sometimes religious believers do use language meaninglessly.

Parable

A member of a resistance movement (a partisan) meets a stranger who says he is in charge of the resistance and talks to him alone for a long time. He is very impressed with the stranger and believes in him completely based on their conversation.

After this, he sometimes observes the stranger helping the resistance, but other times observes the stranger betraying the resistance. He remains convinced that the stranger is on their side.

Similarly, he sometimes asks the stranger for help and gets it, but other times the stranger refuses. He continues to believe that the stranger knows best.

He recognises that the stranger's behaviour sometimes counts against his beliefs. He experiences doubt and conflict about it but keeps faith in the stranger.

He has a reason to keep faith in the stranger based on their first meeting, and his belief that the stranger is on their side explains the stranger's behaviour.

Argument

Religious claims are not "conclusively falsifiable" because a believer, like the member of the resistance, won't allow this.

Some believers don't recognise any evidence against their claims or just blindly assert something like "it is God's will" in the face of natural disasters. This is meaningless use of language and Flew is right here.

However, religious language can be meaningful if believers recognise that there is evidence against them and have good original reasons for their faith.

Therefore: Religious claims are meaningful assertions some of the time, but it is dependent on how believers make those claims.

Strength of Mitchell

Mitchell's account is strong because it is much more balanced than Flew. He arguably presents a more accurate account of what religious belief and language is really like.

Most believers experience strong doubts and acknowledge this in religious language, just as the member of the resistance does in the parable. This makes their language use more meaningful than Flew admits.

Therefore: Mitchell is successful in defending religious language from Flew's criticism.

Criticism of Mitchell

Mitchell's member of the resistance movement is still basically behaving like the believing explorer. He refuses to abandon his belief despite strong evidence that something is not right with the stranger.

The fact that he acknowledges this does not change the fact that there is something irrational about him.

Therefore: Mitchell has failed to show that religious believers use language much more rationally and meaningfully than in Flew's criticism.

3.3.3 HARE: BLIKS AND THE LUNATIC

General note: Hare is broadly on the side of religious believers. He is arguing that religious language is meaningful in some cases because it expresses basic beliefs, and everyone needs basic beliefs so it's not irrational to have them.

Parable

A madman is convinced that all academics want to murder him. He holds this belief despite all attempts to convince him otherwise.

Any time he meets an academic who is respectable and kind, he says that the academic is really plotting against him.

The madman is clearly deluded and allows no evidence to falsify his belief that academics want to murder him.

The madman's belief is unfalsifiable, but it is not the same as no belief at all. It is a blik.

A blik is a basic belief that is held like an axiom - it is something we base our other beliefs on but which we can't justify ourselves.

The madman has an insane blik and we have sane ones.

Argument

We all have bliks. For example, the blik that the future resembles the bast. Hume showed this to be a basic belief rather than something we can prove.

Hence, having a basic belief that you hold which is unfalsifiable is not necessarily meaningless.

Therefore: Religious language sometimes expresses a blik, and such a blik is not meaningless or insane.

Strength of Hare

Things like inductive reasoning (e.g. from the past to the future) or beliefs about what is right and wrong may be impossible to verify or falsify, but they are meaningful and vital to our lives.

By showing that a religious belief is similar to such vital beliefs, Hare is arguably successful in showing that it is meaningful even if Flew is right that it is unfalsifiable.

Criticism of Hare

Hare has not shown that religious belief is a good basic belief to hold or that it is vital to our lives. Just because it is similar to basic beliefs such as induction, this doesn't show that it is just as sane or useful.

Therefore: Hare's response is weak because he cannot show that religious belief is a sane blik. Religious language might be technically meaningful, but could still be quite irrational.

4. NOTES AND REFERENCES

This section includes links to original texts you might want to follow up my presentation of arguments in, and useful quotes that I noted down in the course of writing this book. Some arguments in the syllabus are debatable in the sense that people disagree on how to interpret the original texts. The quotes and references in this section will hopefully show how I've interpreted the texts.

Some sections of the syllabus are fairly common sense, so there isn't a note or reference for everything.

I've tried to put links to any good online texts I could find. I have a feeling that I should include some legal disclaimer about this. Please be aware that you visit these links at your own risk and I'm not responsible for the contents of the websites or anything you download from them.

4.1 THE CONCEPT OF GOD

4.1.1 ETERNALITY

The Eternality article in the AQA Anthology / Resource List is formidably hard to read!

It's also behind a paywall on JSTOR, but I realised it's also available for free at the author's website, unfortunately without page numbers:

https://sites.google.com/site/stumpep/home/onlinepapers

direct link to PDF:

https://drive.google.com/open?id=0Bwre_fqicQ1pUTY3Z0IjOG51Sm8

(Stump, E, Kretzmann, N, Eternity: journal of philosophy, 78 (8):429–458)

When reading the article, I noted the following quotes and pages in the JSTOR version. The quote from p.445 below is in my opinion quite important for understanding the idea that existing in eternity is a more perfect form of existence.

Text without quotation marks is my paraphrase of what it says on that page.

p.433-434: "So whatever has the complete possession of all its life at once cannot be temporal. The life that is the mode of an eternal entity's existence is thus characterized not only by duration but also by atemporality."

p.438: Physics shows that simultaneity is not a feature of reality.

p.443: "What the concept of eternity implies instead is that there is one objective reality that contains two modes of real existence in which two different sorts of duration are measured by two irreducibly different sorts of measure: time and eternity."

P.445: "Atemporal duration is duration none of which is not - none of which is absent (and hence future) or flowed away (and hence past). Eternity, not time, is the mode of existence that admits of fully realized duration."

p.446: God as an atemporal mind which can do certain things:

"Considered as an atemporal mind, God cannot deliberate, anticipate, remember, or plan ahead, for instance; all these mental activities essentially involve time, either in taking time to be performed (like deliberation) or in requiring a temporal viewpoint as a prerequisite to performance (like remembering). But it is clear that there are other mental activities that do not require a temporal interval or viewpoint. Knowing seems to be the paradigm case; learning, reasoning, inferring take time, as knowing does not."

p.446-447 Atemporal minds have awareness, will, feelings of approval or disapproval.

p.448 "If an eternal God is also omnipotent, he can do anything it is not logically impossible for him to do. Even though his actions cannot be located in time, he can bring about effects in time unless doing so is logically im possible for him."

p.450 "If it is not impossible for an omnipotent, eternal entity to act in eternity (by atemporally willing) in such a way as to bring it about that a temporal entity begins to exist at a particular time, it is not impossible for an omnipotent, eternal entity to act in eternity (by atemporally willing) in such a way that that temporal entity continues to exist during a particular temporal interval."

p.457-458 Concept of a perfect being that is eternal is coherent, but not of a perfect being that is temporal.

4.1.2 THE EUTHYTHRO DILEMMA

See https://www.iep.utm.edu/divine-c/#SH4a for Alston's response in more detail.

4.2 ARGUMENTS FOR THE EXISTENCE OF GOD

4.2.1 THE ONTOLOGICAL ARGUMENT

I used this website to read Anselm and Gaunilo:

https://sourcebooks.fordham.edu/basis/anselm-proslogium.asp

Kant's Objection to the Ontological Argument

I found the Critique of Pure Reason section where this appears surprisingly easy to read, at least in the English translation! I'd assumed Kant would be very difficult to decode, but found his writing remarkably clear, almost like Hume.

This link should take you to the page where he starts to criticise the ontological argument:

https://archive.org/details/immanuelkantscri032379mbp/page/n521

Here (p.505 in the book) is the somewhat famous reference to 100 Thalers:

https://archive.org/details/immanuelkantscri032379mbp/page/n525

"A hundred real thalers do not contain the least coin more than a hundred possible thalers."

4.2.2 THE TELEOLOGICAL ARGUMENT

Paley's Teleological argument

Paley's book can be found in its entirety here:

http://darwin-online.org.uk/content/frameset?itemID=A142&pageseq=1&viewtype=text

The problem of spatial disorder

Oddly, neither Hume nor Paley use the phrase 'Spatial disorder'. The people who wrote the AQA syllabus appear to have taken it from the 1968 article by Swinburne in which he uses this phrase.

Swinburne himself doesn't provide an exact reference to a relevant passage in Hume. He presents the problem as follows in his article:

Swinburne, R G (1968), The argument from design, Philosophy 43 (165), 199-212

p.201: "... although the world contains many striking regularities of copresence (some few of which are due to human agency), it also contains many examples of spatial disorder. The uniform distribution of the galactic clusters is a marvellous example of spatial order, but the arrangement of trees in an African jungle is a marvellous example of spatial disorder. Although the proponent of the argument may then proceed to argue that in an important sense or from some point of view (e.g. utility to man) the order vastly exceeds the disorder, he has to argue for this in no way obvious proposition."

I can't find a single point where Hume presents spatial disorder as a distinct objection, and, confusingly, Swinburne doesn't include spatial disorder in his list on pp. 207 - 211 of all of the Humean criticisms he could find. Below are the best passages I could find in Hume's Dialogues for it:

In Part 4 of the Dialogues, Hume has this sentence:

"We have also experience of particular systems of thought and of matter which have no order; of the first in madness, of the second in corruption. Why, then, should we think, that order is more essential to one than the other? And if it requires a cause in both, what do we gain by your system, in tracing the universe of objects into a similar universe of ideas? "

In Part 5 disorder is again touched on:

"There are many inexplicable difficulties in the works of Nature, which, if we allow a perfect author to be proved a priori, are easily solved, and become only seeming difficulties, from the narrow capacity of man, who cannot trace infinite relations. But according to your method of reasoning, these difficulties become all real; and perhaps will be insisted on, as new instances of likeness to human art and contrivance. At least, you must acknowledge, that it is impossible for us to tell, from our limited views, whether this system contains any great faults, or deserves any considerable praise, if compared to other possible, and even real systems. Could a peasant, if the Aeneid were read to him, pronounce that poem to be absolutely faultless, or even assign to it its proper rank among the productions of human wit, he, who had never seen any other production? "

In Part 8 Hume refers to disorder again, although more in the context of the Epicurean hypothesis:

"A defect in any of these particulars destroys the form; and the matter of which it is composed is again set loose, and is thrown into irregular motions and fermentations, till it unite itself to some other regular form. If no such form be prepared to receive it, and if there be a great quantity of this corrupted matter in the universe, the universe itself is entirely disordered; whether it be the feeble embryo of a world in its first beginnings that is thus destroyed, or the rotten carcass of one languishing in old age and infirmity. In either case, a chaos ensues; till finite, though innumerable revolutions produce at last some forms, whose parts and organs are so adjusted as to support the forms amidst a continued succession of matter. "

For Paley, this seems to be where he responds, on pp. 4-6 of Natural Theology:

"II. Neither, secondly, would it invalidate our conclusion, that the watch sometimes went wrong, or that it seldom went exactly right. The purpose of the machinery, the design, and the designer, might be evident, and in the case supposed would be evident, in whatever way we accounted for the irregularity of the movement, or whether we could account for it or not. It is not necessary that a machine be perfect, in order to show with what design it was made: still less necessary, where the only question is, whether it were made with any design at all.

III. Nor, thirdly, would it bring any uncertainty into the argument, if there were a few parts of the watch, concerning which we could not discover, or had not yet discovered, in what manner they conduced to the general effect; or even some parts, concerning which we could not ascertain, whether they conduced to that effect in any manner whatever. For, as to the first branch of the case; if by the loss, or disorder, or decay of the parts in question, the movement of the watch were found in fact to be stopped, or disturbed, or retarded, no doubt would remain in our minds as to the utility or intention of these parts, although we should be unable to investigate the manner according to which, or the connexion by which, the ultimate effect depended upon their action or assistance; and the more complex is the machine, the more likely is this obscurity to arise. Then, as to the second thing supposed, namely, that there were parts which might be spared, without prejudice to the movement of the watch, and that we had proved this by experiment,–these superfluous parts, even if we were completely assured that they were such, would not vacate the reasoning which we had instituted concerning other parts. The indication of contrivance remained, with respect to them, nearly as it was before. "

4.2.3 THE COSMOLOGICAL ARGUMENT

Descartes' Cosmological Argument

This was one of the most difficult parts of the book to write. It is not presented very clearly in the original text, in my humble opinion!

In this section, you can trace my rendering of his argument back to the original text, sentence by sentence.

I used this website which uses a somewhat old translation:
http://www.classicallibrary.org/descartes/meditations/6.htm

The great advantage of the text I used is that it has clear divisions into short paragraphs.

Below I've put a reference to Descartes' individual paragraphs (from the text above) from the Meditations next to each of the premises and conclusion as I've expressed them that are in the main part of this book.

I exist and I clearly conceive an idea of God as an infinite, eternal, perfect, being. This idea is distinct from all other ideas about finite things. (3:5 - 3:13)

The efficient cause of something must have as much reality as the effect. Otherwise, the effect would not be real. (3:14)

The idea of God, unlike ideas of people, angels, imaginary creatures, cannot possibly come from my own mind, because I do not have the perfections it contains and I am not infinite. (3:22 - 3:27)

I cannot have created myself, because I would have given myself all possible knowledge and perfections (3:29-30)

There cannot be an infinite regress of causes that led to me, because this would not explain my continuing existence. (3:34)

My ultimate cause cannot be multiple things, because unity and simplicity is part of the perfection of God, and (as above), the cause must have at least as much reality as the effect. (3:35)

Therefore, my continued existence as a thinking thing possessing the idea of God can only be explained by the existence of a perfect, necessary, and infinite being which is both the cause and sustainer of my existence. (3:33 - 3:36)

The AQA suggested version of Meditations 3 is:
http://www.earlymoderntexts.com/assets/pdfs/descartes1641_2.pdf

Hume's objection to the 'causal principle'

Wikisource is a most useful website, and has the section of the Treatise where Hume discusses causality here:

https://en.wikisource.org/wiki/Treatise_of_Human_Nature/Book_1:_Of_the_understanding/Part_3/Section_3

I find this quote particularly important as a summary:

"But this does not prove, that every being must be preceded by a cause; no more than it follows, because every husband must have a wife, that therefore every man must be marry'd. The true state of the question is, whether every object, which begins to exist, must owe its existence to a cause; and this I assert neither to be intuitively nor demonstratively certain, and hope to have prov'd it sufficiently by the foregoing arguments."

Hume's argument on necessary beings

Wikisource has the relevant section of the Dialogues here:

https://en.wikisource.org/wiki/Dialogues_Concerning_Natural_Religion/Part_9

The following quote is found around the middle of the page:

"I shall begin with observing, that there is an evident absurdity in pretending to demonstrate a matter of fact, or to prove it by any arguments a priori. Nothing is demonstrable, unless the contrary implies a contradiction. Nothing, that is distinctly conceivable, implies a contradiction. Whatever we conceive as existent, we can also conceive as non-existent. There is no being, therefore, whose non-existence implies a contradiction. Consequently there is no being, whose existence is demonstrable. I propose this argument as entirely decisive, and am willing to rest the whole controversy upon it."

4.3 RELIGIOUS LANGUAGE

4.3.1 VERIFICATIONISM

I noted down the following quotes from Language Truth and Logic, which I'm guessing is out of copyright. I used this edition:

http://s-f-walker.org.uk/pubsebooks/pdfs/ayerLTL.pdf

The criterion itself:

LTL Chapter 1, page 6
"The criterion which we use to test the genuineness of apparent statements of fact is the criterion of verifiability. We say that a sentence is factually significant to any given person, if, and only if, he knows how to verify the proposition which it purports to express—that is, if he knows what observations would lead him, under certain conditions, to accept the proposition as being true, or reject it as being false. "

Verification in practice versus principle:

pp.6-7
"In the first place, it is necessary to draw a distinction between practical verifiability, and verifiability in principle. Plainly we all understand, in many cases believe, propositions which we have not in fact taken steps to verify. Many of these are propositions which we could verify if we took enough trouble. But there remain a number of significant propositions, concerning matters of fact, which we could not verify even if we chose; simply because we lack the practical means of placing ourselves in the situation where the relevant observations could be made. A simple and familiar example of such a proposition is the proposition that there are mountains on the farther side of themoon. No rocket has yet been invented which would enable me to go and look at the farther side of the moon, so that I am unable to decide the matter by actual observation. But I do know what observations would decide it for me. if, as is theoretically conceivable. I were once in a position to make them. And therefore I say that the proposition is verifiable in principle, if not in practice, and is accordingly significant. "

Strong and weak verification:

p.7

"A further distinction which we must make is the distinction between the 'strong' and the 'weak' sense of the term 'verifiable'. A proposition is said to be verifiable, in the strong sense of the term, if. and only if, its truth could be conclusively established in experience. But it is verifiable. in the weak sense, if it is possible for experience to render it probable."

This quote is good to read because it clearly distinguishes verificationism from atheism or agnosticism:

Chapter 6, page 73 - 74

"It is important not to confuse this view of religious assertions with the view that is adopted by atheists, or agnostics. For it is characteristic of an agnostic to hold that the existence of a god is a possibility in which there is no good reason either to believe or disbelieve; and it is characteristic of an atheist to hold that it is at least probable that no god exists. And our view that all utterances about the nature of God are nonsensical, so far from being identical with, or even lending any support to, either of these familiar contentions, is actually incompatible with them. For if the assertion that there is a god is nonsensical, then the atheist's assertion that there is no god is equally nonsensical, since it is only a significant proposition that can be significantly contradicted. As for the agnostic, although he refrains from saying either that there is or that there is not a god, he does not deny that the question whether a transcendent god exists is a genuine question."

4.3.2 ESCHATOLOGICAL VERIFICATION

Hick's books are not easily available online, but I found a way to read his Eschatological Verification argument in the original without having to go to a library.

It's in his "Philosophy of Religion" book. The AQA scheme of work suggests that E.V. appears in "Evil and the God of Love", but I can't any reference to it in the edition I read.

If you go here:

https://archive.org/details/philosophyofreli00hick

and set up a free account, you can legally (I think) borrow the book online for 14 days. Eschatological Verification is found in Chapter 7 and is presented in a few handily numbered points, unlike the Irenaean Theodicy!

When I looked at the contents page of Hick's "Philosophy of Religion" I was struck by its similarity to many A Level syllabi through the years, right down to the order in which the different areas are covered. I'm sure this is just a coincidence!

4.3.3 THE UNIVERSITY DEBATE

Flew, Antony, Richard M Hare and Basil Mitchell (1955), 'Theology and Falsification' in New Essays in Philosophical Theology, edited by Antony Flew and Alasdair MacIntyre, London, SMC Press

http://www.politik-salon.de/files/theory_of_falsification.pdf

Note: The PDF available from politik-salon.de (the personal website of a German Economics professor) is of unknown origin and has many small typos, perhaps because it was scanned and then converted to text by optical character recognition (OCR) software. Sadly this seems to be pretty much the only openly available PDF version of the article. Note that Hare really does refer to Muslims as 'Mussulmans' (!), which was still normal in the 1950s, and not intended to be derogatory in this case.

Printed in Great Britain
by Amazon